W9-AVH-067

EDGE BOOKS™

COPILOT

LEVEL 2

PAPER AIRPLANES

BY CHRISTOPHER L. HARBO

TABLE OF

contents

Time to Fly

Welcome to the cockpit! You've passed flight school and earned your seat next to the pilot. Now it's time to get a feel for those flight controls. Nine airplanes need your help getting airborne.

Level 2

Your first task in the copilot seat is to practice your folding skills. The instructions for these models aren't too difficult. Just remember to make your folds cleanly and crisply. In no time, your paper gliders will be soaring all over the neighborhood.

materials

Every paper airplane builder needs a well-stocked toolbox. The models in this book use the materials listed below. Take a minute before you begin folding to gather what you need:

 **PAPER** — Any paper you can fold will work. Notebook paper is always popular. But paper with cool colors and designs gives your planes style.

 SCISSORS — Keep a scissors handy. Some models need a snip here or there to fly well.

 **RUBBER BANDS** — Rubber bands can send some airplane models sailing. Long, thin rubber bands work well.

 **PAPER CLIPS** — Paper clips are perfect for adding weight to a plane's nose. Keep a supply of small and large paper clips on hand.

 **CLEAR TAPE** — Most paper airplanes don't need tape. But when they do, you'll be glad you have it ready to go.

Techniques and Terms

Folding paper airplanes isn't difficult when you understand common folding techniques and terms. Review this list before folding the models in this book. Remember to refer back to this list if you get stuck on a tricky step.

VALLEY FOLDS

Valley folds are represented by a dashed line. The paper is creased along the line. The top surface of the paper is folded against itself like a book.

MOUNTAIN FOLDS

Mountain folds are represented by a pink or white dashed and dotted line. The paper is creased along the line and folded behind.

REVERSE FOLDS

Reverse folds are made by opening a pocket slightly and folding the model inside itself along existing creases.

Mark folds are light folds used to make reference creases for a later step. Ideally, a mark fold will not be seen in the finished model.

RABBIT ear FOLDS

Rabbit ear folds are formed by bringing two edges of a point together using existing creases. The new point is folded to one side.

SQUASH FOLDS

Squash folds are formed by lifting one edge of a pocket and reforming it so the spine gets flattened. The existing creases become new edges.

FOLDING SYMBOLS

Fold the paper in the direction of the arrow.

Fold the paper behind.

Fold the paper and then unfold it.

Turn the paper over or rotate it to a new position.

A fold or edge hidden under another layer of paper; also used to mark where to cut with a scissors

Air Shark

Prowl the skies with your very own Air Shark. This sturdy plane has a smooth, steady glide. It's a paper predator that's always ready to hunt.

MATERIALS

* 8.5- by 11-inch (22- by 28-centimeter) paper

Start Here

1 Valley fold edge to edge and unfold.

2 Valley fold the corners to the center.

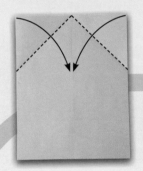

3 Turn the paper over.

4 Valley fold the edges to the center. Allow the flaps behind to release to the top.

END HERE

9 Finished Air Shark

8 Lift the wings.

7 Valley fold the top layer even with the bottom edge. Repeat behind.

FLYING TIP

Use a medium, level throw.

5 Mountain fold the point.

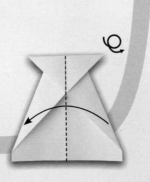

6 Valley fold the model in half and rotate.

9

WIND Tunnel

TRADITIONAL MODEL

The Wind Tunnel takes paper airplanes in a very different direction. This circular wing is thrown like a football. Get your arm warmed up. You'll be amazed by how far this tube will glide through the air.

materials

- 8.5- by 11-inch (22- by 28-cm) paper
- scissors
- tape

Start Here

2 Valley fold the edge to create a narrow strip.

1 Cut the paper in half the long way. Use one half for step 2.

4 Shape the tube into a smooth circle.

3 Tape the seam to hold the model together.

10

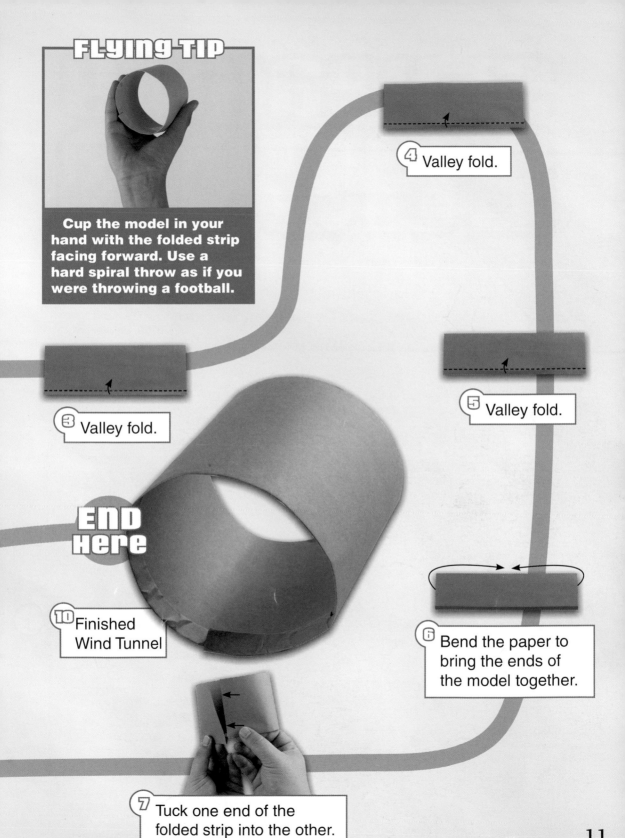

Cup the model in your hand with the folded strip facing forward. Use a hard spiral throw as if you were throwing a football.

④ Valley fold.

⑤ Valley fold.

③ Valley fold.

END HERE

⑩ Finished Wind Tunnel

⑥ Bend the paper to bring the ends of the model together.

⑦ Tuck one end of the folded strip into the other.

streaking EAGLE

The Streaking Eagle combines style and mechanics. Sleek wing flaps help the plane fly straight. Elevator flaps let you control how the plane rises or dives.

materials

* 8.5- by 11-inch (22- by 28-cm) paper
* scissors

9 Cut a flap in the back of each wing. Angle the flaps upward slightly.

END Here

10 Finished Streaking Eagle

FLYING TIP

Use a medium, level throw. Adjust the elevator flaps to control the flight path.

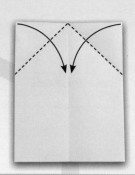

1. Valley fold edge to edge and unfold.

2. Valley fold the corners to the center.

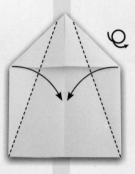

3. Valley fold the corners to the center and rotate.

8. Lift the wing flaps so they stand up at 90-degree angles.

7. Lift the wings.

4. Valley fold in half.

6. Valley fold the edge of the wing. Repeat behind.

5. Valley fold the top layer. Repeat behind.

13

parakeet

The Parakeet is a little plane with a lot of attitude. This feisty model doesn't bother with a straight flight. It prefers to swoop, dive, and curve through the air. Each flight is a new adventure.

materials

* 6-inch (15-cm) square of paper

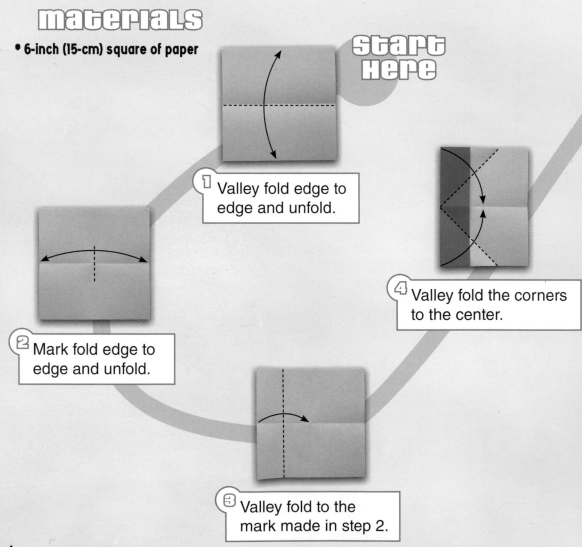

start Here

1 Valley fold edge to edge and unfold.

2 Mark fold edge to edge and unfold.

3 Valley fold to the mark made in step 2.

4 Valley fold the corners to the center.

14

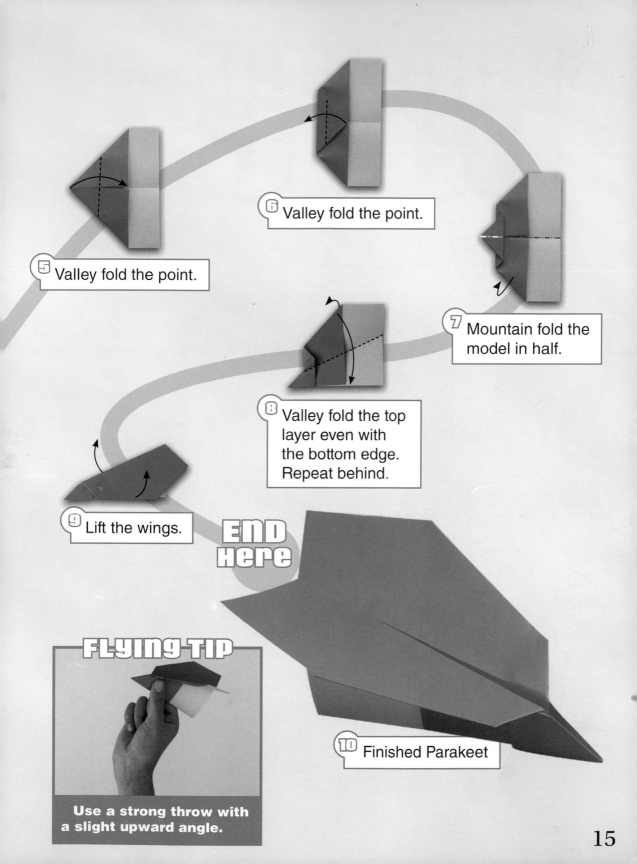

5 Valley fold the point.

6 Valley fold the point.

7 Mountain fold the model in half.

8 Valley fold the top layer even with the bottom edge. Repeat behind.

9 Lift the wings.

END HERE

FLYING TIP

10 Finished Parakeet

Use a strong throw with a slight upward angle.

15

WHISPER Dart

DESIGNED BY CHRISTOPHER L. HARBO

The Whisper Dart has a secret. It looks like a simple paper airplane. But a couple of extra folds give it added weight in the nose. Do you have your eye on a target across the room? This design will deliver!

materials

• 8.5- by 11-inch (22- by 28-cm) paper

start Here

1 Valley fold edge to edge and unfold.

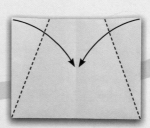

2 Valley fold the corners to the center. Note how the creases end at the bottom corners of the paper.

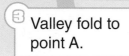

3 Valley fold to point A.

4 Valley fold.

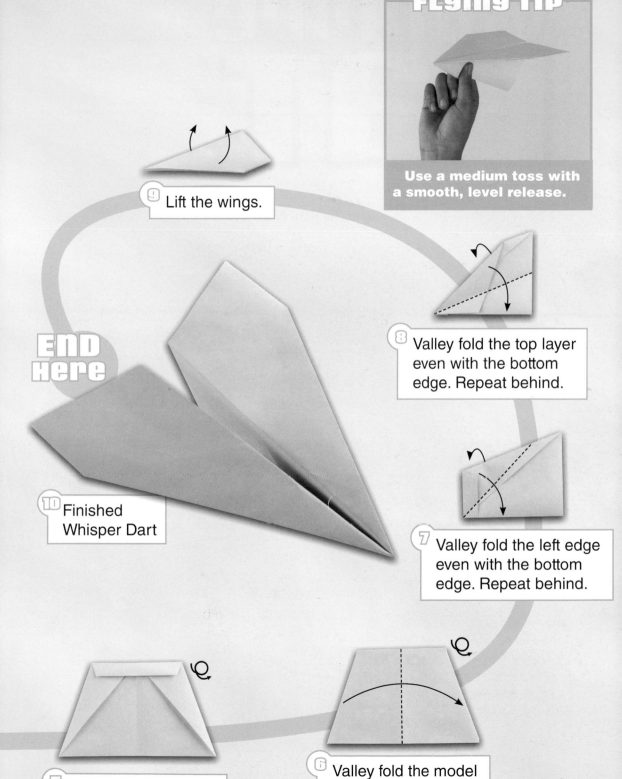

Use a medium toss with a smooth, level release.

9 Lift the wings.

8 Valley fold the top layer even with the bottom edge. Repeat behind.

END HERE

7 Valley fold the left edge even with the bottom edge. Repeat behind.

10 Finished Whisper Dart

5 Turn the model over.

6 Valley fold the model in half and rotate.

17

vampire BAT

TRADITIONAL MODEL

The Vampire Bat's flight path is a jaw-dropper. This amazing wing soars and swoops when thrown correctly. Folding it is easy. Finding a room large enough to fly it in may be a challenge.

materials

* 8.5- by 11-inch (22- by 28-cm) paper

Start Here

1 Valley fold edge to edge and unfold.

2 Valley fold the top edge so it rests about 2 inches (5 cm) from the bottom edge.

3 Valley fold the corners to the center and unfold.

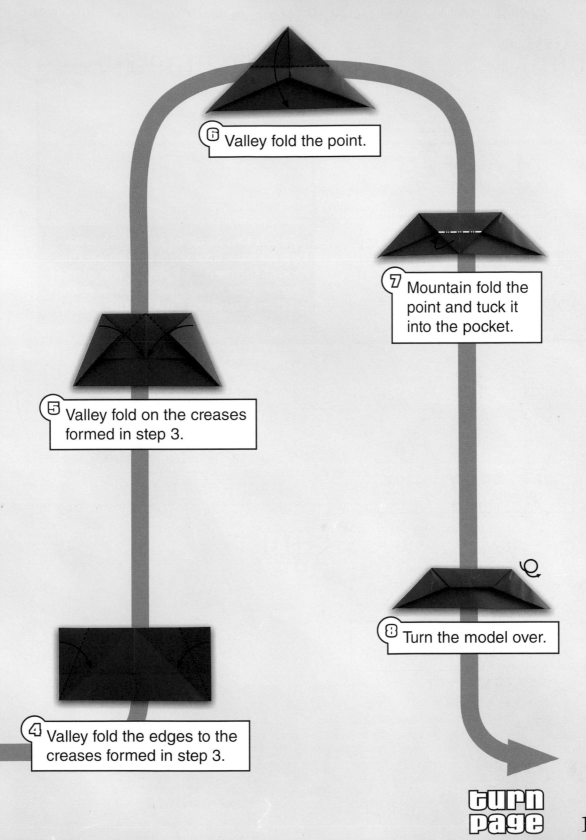

6 Valley fold the point.

7 Mountain fold the point and tuck it into the pocket.

5 Valley fold on the creases formed in step 3.

8 Turn the model over.

4 Valley fold the edges to the creases formed in step 3.

turn page

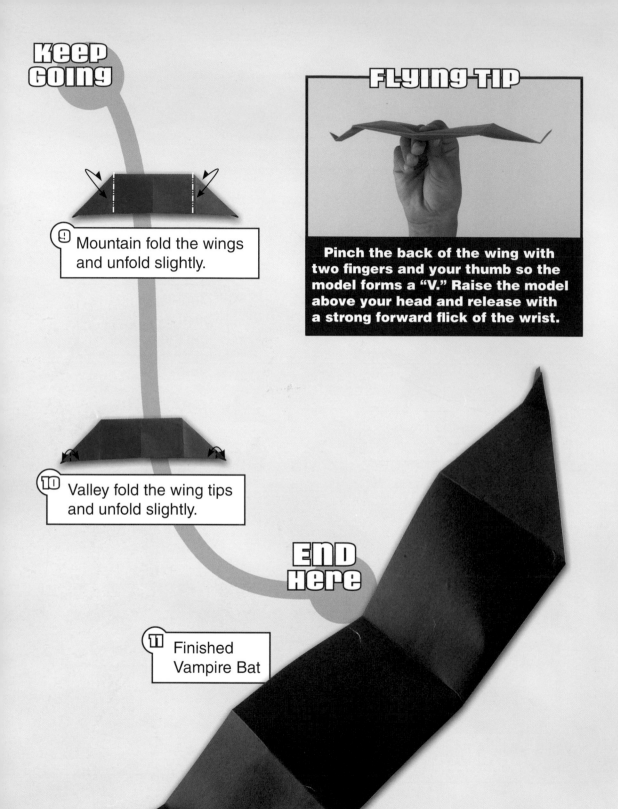

FLYING TIP

Pinch the back of the wing with two fingers and your thumb so the model forms a "V." Raise the model above your head and release with a strong forward flick of the wrist.

9 Mountain fold the wings and unfold slightly.

10 Valley fold the wing tips and unfold slightly.

END HERE

11 Finished Vampire Bat

ARROWHEAD

TRADITIONAL MODEL

Get ready to soar! The Arrowhead is a flying champion. This plane can cover amazing distances with very little effort. You'll get your exercise chasing this model from one end of the room to the other.

materials

• 8.5- by 11-inch (22- by 28-cm) paper

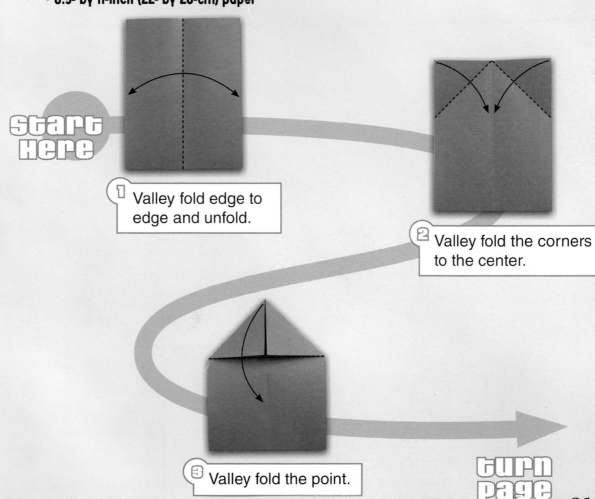

start here

1 Valley fold edge to edge and unfold.

2 Valley fold the corners to the center.

3 Valley fold the point.

turn page

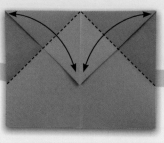

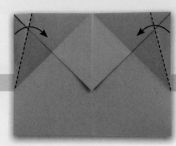

4 Valley fold the corners to the center and unfold.

5 Valley fold the corners. Note that the creases end at the creases made in step 4.

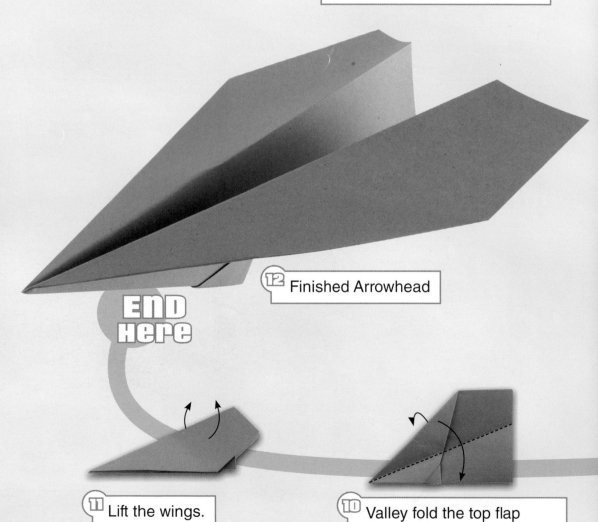

12 Finished Arrowhead

END
Here

11 Lift the wings.

10 Valley fold the top flap even with the bottom edge. Repeat behind.

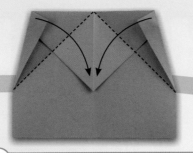

6 Valley fold on the creases made in step 4.

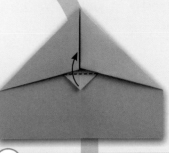

7 Valley fold the point.

8 Turn the model over.

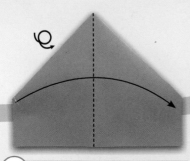

9 Valley fold the model in half and rotate.

NIGHTHAWK

TRADITIONAL MODEL

The Nighthawk is a great flier with a simple design. This classic glider isn't fancy, but its graceful flight is sure to impress. Make two planes and challenge a friend to a flight contest.

materials

* 8.5- by 11-inch (22- by 28-cm) paper

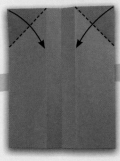

4 Valley fold the corners to the creases made in step 2.

5 Valley fold the point.

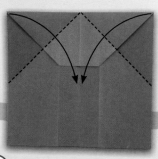

6 Valley fold the corners to the center crease.

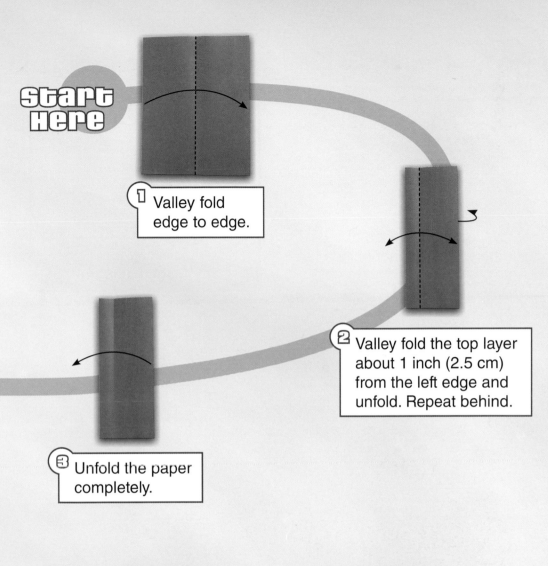

start here

1 Valley fold edge to edge.

2 Valley fold the top layer about 1 inch (2.5 cm) from the left edge and unfold. Repeat behind.

3 Unfold the paper completely.

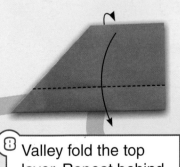

7 Valley fold the model in half and rotate.

8 Valley fold the top layer. Repeat behind.

turn page

9 Valley fold the edge of the wing. Repeat behind.

10 Lift the wings.

11 Lift the wing flaps so they stand up at 90-degree angles.

END
HERE

12 Finished Nighthawk

26

vapor

DESIGNED BY CHRISTOPHER L. HARBO

The Vapor has extra folds in the nose for strength and balance. The wing flaps guide the plane on an even flight. With very little effort, this model will slip silently from your hand and arc across the room.

materials

* 8.5- by 11-inch (22- by 28-cm) paper

start here

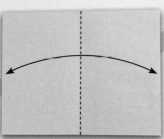

1 Valley fold edge to edge and unfold.

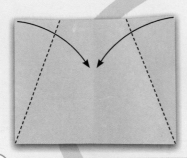

2 Valley fold the corners to the center. Note how the creases end at the bottom corners of the paper.

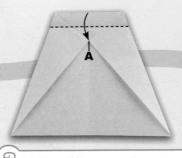

3 Valley fold to point A.

turn page

27

Keep Going

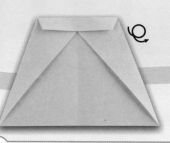

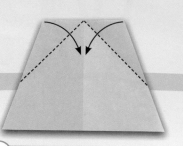

4 Turn the model over.

5 Valley fold the corners to the center.

8 Valley fold the edge of the wing. Repeat behind.

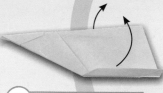

9 Lift the wings.

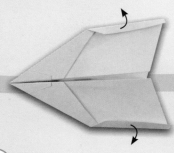

10 Lift the wing flaps so they stand up at 90-degree angles.

6 Valley fold the model in half and rotate.

FLYING TIP

Use a medium, smooth throw with a slight upward angle.

7 Valley fold the top layer. Repeat behind.

END Here

11 Finished Vapor

29

BULLS-EYE

How accurate is your aim? Find out by challenging a friend to a game of Bulls-eye!

materials

- twine
- hula hoop
- masking tape
- 2 paper airplanes
- pencil
- notepad

WHAT YOU DO

1. Tie one end of a piece of twine to a hula hoop.

2. Tape the other end of the twine to the top of an open door frame. Allow the hoop to hang about 4 feet (1.2 meters) off the ground. If the hoop is too large for the doorway, simply allow it to straddle the door frame.

3. Walk 15 to 20 steps away from the hoop and turn around. Mark this spot on the floor with a piece of tape. The tape marks your throwing line.

4. Take turns throwing your paper airplanes from the throwing line. Planes that fly through the hoop score 5 points. Planes that fly above or below the hoop and through the doorway score 3 points. Planes that fail to pass through the hoop or the doorway receive no points.

5. Write down your scores on the notepad after each throw. After each player throws 10 times, add up the scores. The player with the highest score is the Bulls-eye champion!

Read More

Dewar, Andrew. *Fun and Easy Paper Airplanes.* North Clarendon, Vt.: Tuttle Publishing, 2008.

Harbo, Christopher L. *The Kids' Guide to Paper Airplanes.* Kids' Guides. Mankato, Minn.: Capstone Press, 2009.

Mitchell, David. *Paper Airplanes: How to Make Them and Fly Them.* New York: Sterling Publishing, 2005.

Internet Sites

FactHound offers a safe, fun way to find Internet sites related to this book. All of the sites on FactHound have been researched by our staff.

Here's all you do:

Visit *www.facthound.com*

Type in this code: 9781429647427

Edge Books are published by Capstone Press,
151 Good Counsel Drive, P.O. Box 669, Mankato, Minnesota 56002.
www.capstonepub.com

 Books published by Capstone Press are manufactured with paper containing at least 10 percent post-consumer waste.

Library of Congress Cataloging-in-Publication Data
Harbo, Christopher L.
  Paper airplanes, Copilot level 2 / by Christopher L. Harbo.
    p. cm.—(Edge books. Paper airplanes)
  Includes bibliographical references.
  Summary: "Provides instructions and photo-illustrated diagrams for making a
    variety of traditional and original paper airplanes"—Provided by publisher.
  ISBN 978-1-4296-4742-7 (library binding)
  1. Paper airplanes—Juvenile literature. I. Title. II. Series.

TL778.H3733 2011
745.592—dc22   2010001004

Editorial Credits
Kyle Grenz, designer; Marcie Spence, media researcher; Marcy Morin, scheduler;
    Laura Manthe, production specialist

Photo Credits
Capstone Studio/Karon Dubke, all planes and steps
Shutterstock/newphotoservice, cover (background); Serg64, cover (background)